MINES OF DIFFICULTY

MINES OF DIFFICULTY

A COMMENTARY ON FIRST AND SECOND THESSALONIANS

DOUGLAS WILSON

Douglas Wilson, *Mines of Difficulty: A Commentary on First and Second Thessalonians*
Copyright © 2022 by Douglas Wilson

Published by Canon Press
P. O. Box 8729, Moscow, Idaho 83843
800–488–2034 | www.canonpress.com

Cover design by James Engerbretson
Interior design by Valerie Anne Bost
Printed in the United States of America

All rights reserved. No part of this publication may be reproduced, stored in a retrieval system, or transmitted in any form by any means, electronic, mechanical, photocopy, recording, or otherwise, without prior permission of the author, except as provided by USA copyright law.

All Scripture quotations are from the King James Version.

Library of Congress Cataloging-in-Publication Data forthcoming

23 24 25 26 27 28 29 30 31   10 9 8 7 6 5 4 3 2 1

CONTENTS

1 THESSALONIANS

INTRODUCTION
3

1 THESSALONIANS 1
9

1 THESSALONIANS 2
15

1 THESSALONIANS 3
27

1 THESSALONIANS 4
37

1 THESSALONIANS 5
49

2 THESSALONIANS

INTRODUCTION
61

2 THESSALONIANS 1
65

2 THESSALONIANS 2
75

2 THESSALONIANS 3
85

To Ethan Oldham,
who creates the kind of editorial difficulties
that keep me out of difficulties.

1 THESSALONIANS

INTRODUCTION

Thessalonica was a principal city in Macedonia, the region that was the home of Philip and the great Alexander. This letter was written around AD 50, which would make it, with the exception of Galatians, the earliest record of Paul's writing. While the Jews in Berea were more noble than the Jews in Thessalonica (Acts 17:11), the *church* in Thessalonica was in many respects one of Paul's success stories. The Christians there were noble.

The three great emphases of 1 Thessalonians are *chastity* in sexual matters, *diligence* in work, and intelligent fervency in eschatological *hope*. Overarching everything else in both of these letters are the questions of a surrounding eschatology, and we can see that however fervent Paul was in his eschatological hope, he was unbending in his understanding that such hope had ethical corollaries: do *not* be unchaste and do *not* be lazy.

He concludes the letter with a benediction, calling upon the God of peace to sanctify the Thessalonians entirely. He prays that this sanctification unto blamelessness would be extensive in their persons (spirit, soul, body), which would include their sexual behavior, and also extensive in time (until the *parousia* of the Lord Jesus).

The church at Thessalonica was a thriving one, but like many busy places there were a number of free riders. This letter and the next letter to the Thessalonians both address the problem of shiftlessness. Slackers and sponges had to be dealt with firmly.

Paul began his work in Thessalonica by setting a good example: "For ye remember, brethren, our *labour and travail*: for *labouring night and day*, because we would not be chargeable unto any of you, we preached unto you the gospel of God" (2:9).

He also established leaders in the church who would continue with that same good example: "And we beseech you, brethren, to know them *which labour among you*, and are over you in the Lord, and admonish you; And to esteem them very highly in love *for their work's sake*. And be at peace among yourselves" (5:12–13).

In that context, he now delivers a command: "We beseech you, brethren, that ye increase more and more; And that ye study to be quiet, and to do your own business, and to work with your own hands, as we commanded you; That ye may walk honestly toward them that are without, and that ye may have lack of nothing" (4:10–12).

Paul's exhortation regarding chastity is also hard-hitting:

> For this is the will of God, even your sanctification, that ye should abstain from fornication: That every one of you should know how to possess his vessel in sanctification and honour; Not in the lust of concupiscence, even as the Gentiles which know not God: That no man go beyond and defraud his brother in any matter: because that the Lord is the avenger of all such, as we also have forewarned you and testified. For God hath not called us unto uncleanness, but unto holiness. He therefore that despiseth, despiseth not man, but God, who hath also given unto us his holy Spirit. (4:3–8)

There are at least three things to be taken away from this. First, Paul is not offering Christian sexlessness over against pagan sexuality. He says that Christians must learn how to possess their own bodies in *this* way, not in *that* way. The way we are to avoid is the sexuality of atheism.

Second, we need to know what we are rejecting: the passion of lust as exhibited by those who do not know God. The world's approach to sex is demented, but it is a demented caricature of certain creational realities. Men and women are convex and concave in their desires. Men want to possess and women want to be possessed. Men want to want and women want to be wanted. We reject the world's approach to sex by embracing God's approach.

Third, to reject God's pattern here is not to despise men, but rather to despise God. You might *defraud* your brother in this, but it is *God* you are despising.

And as we come to consider the apocalyptic component to all this, we need to divide the subject in two. The Bible teaches that there is a general resurrection at the end of the world—which is what we see described in chapter 4:13–18. Whenever you see the resurrection of the dead being discussed, that is a strong indicator that we are talking about the end of the world. This is the last day that Martha referred to when talking with Jesus about Lazarus (John 11:24).

Take for example chapter three, verse thirteen: "To the end he may stablish your hearts unblameable in holiness before God, even our Father, at the coming of our Lord Jesus Christ with all his saints." Or chapter four, verse fourteen: "For if we believe that Jesus died and rose again, even so them also which sleep in Jesus will God bring with him."

We are plainly not talking about the destruction of Jerusalem here—it is way too noisy. One verse pretty much sums it up: "For the Lord himself shall descend from heaven with a shout, with the voice of the archangel, and with the trump of God: and the dead in Christ shall rise first" (4:16).

But this does not mean that the destruction of Jerusalem is not discussed in this letter. No, it is: "And to wait for his Son from heaven, whom he raised from the dead, even Jesus, which delivered us from the wrath to come" (1:10). In chapter 2, Paul compares the persecution that the Thessalonian Christians received to the treatment that the Christians in Judea received, and then he says this: "Forbidding us to speak to the Gentiles that they might be saved, to fill up their sins alway: for the wrath is come upon them to the uttermost" (2:16). That wrath is just around the corner—the day of the Lord, which should be distinguished from the *parousia*.

And so what does this mean? It means that we must return to our text. We pray to God that we would be made *holy and blameless*, being fashioned after the image of Jesus Christ.

1 THESSALONIANS 1

MUCH ASSURANCE IN TROUBLE
The Thessalonians had been called to go through "much affliction" while they were still very young Christians. It is Paul's purpose in this section to remind them of how well they had done, and to explain to them how the grace that had been given to them was a great source of encouragement to saints elsewhere. Paul exults in this because the grace of such courage is contagious.

> Paul, and Silvanus, and Timotheus, unto the church of the Thessalonians which is in God the Father and in the Lord Jesus Christ: Grace be unto you, and peace, from God our Father, and the Lord Jesus Christ.

> We give thanks to God always for you all, making mention of you in our prayers; Remembering without ceasing your work of faith, and labour of love, and patience of hope in our Lord Jesus Christ, in the sight of God and our Father; Knowing, brethren beloved, your election of God. For our gospel came not unto you in word only, but also in power, and in the Holy Ghost, and in much assurance; as ye know what manner of men we were among you for your sake. And ye became followers of us, and of the Lord, having received the word in much affliction, with joy of the Holy Ghost: So that ye were ensamples to all that believe in Macedonia and Achaia. For from you sounded out the word of the Lord not only in Macedonia and Achaia, but also in every place your faith to God-ward is spread abroad; so that we need not to speak any thing. For they themselves shew of us what manner of entering in we had unto you, and how ye turned to God from idols to serve the living and true God; And to wait for his Son from heaven, whom he raised from the dead, even Jesus, which delivered us from the wrath to come. (1 Thess. 1:1–10)

Paul begins with his standard greeting of grace and peace, but in this he is joined by Timothy and Silvanas, who is most likely Silas (v. 1). The church of the Thessalonians was located in God the Father, and in the Lord Jesus Christ (v. 1). Paul always gave thanks to God for them in his prayers (v. 2), never forgetting what a hard-working bunch of Christians they were in the sight of God (v. 3). They were characterized by the work of faith, the labor of love, and the patience of hope. Paul was confident of their election by God (v. 4). Not only did he know their work, he was confident that they also knew *his* work. They knew what kind of men made up Paul's entourage. The gospel came to them, not just in words, but in power, in the Spirit, and *in much assurance* (v. 5). They decided to follow Paul's band, and the Lord also, having received the word in much affliction (v. 6). Notice that the same word is used to describe *much* assurance and *much* affliction. The two go together. This is part of God's routine. What the devil wants to use to unsettle us, God uses to settle us.

The Thessalonians also received the word in the joy of the Holy Spirit, which is fitting (v. 6). They were good examples to all believers throughout Macedonia and Achaia (v. 7), which were northern and southern Greece respectively. Word about their faith had spread even past Greece to regions beyond (v. 8). As a result, Paul did not need to say anything—other people were telling the story of how the Thessalonians received him, and how they turned from idols to the living God (v. 9). The Thessalonians had also been taught to wait for the Son from heaven, the same one whom God raised from the dead, and who delivered us all from the wrath to come (v. 10). Remember there is a connection here—much assurance and coming wrath.

When Paul and Silas first came to Thessalonica, they had gone to the synagogue of the Jews, and Paul had reasoned with the Jews there for three consecutive sabbath days. He reasoned with them from the Scriptures, showing how it was necessary for the Christ to suffer and rise from the dead, and that Jesus of Nazareth was in fact that same Christ. Some of the Jews had believed, and a lot of the Greeks, and more than a few of the leading women in the city. So *these* were the people that Paul is writing to in our letter (Acts 17:1–4).

But the unbelieving Jews in Thessalonica were moved with envy, and so they got some unsavory fellows from Rent-a-Mob, and soon set the whole city in an uproar. Hard to believe, I know, but whole towns can get in a churn. They hauled Jason and some other brothers in front of the rulers of the city. They made some jumbled accusations, enough to trouble the city rulers. The officials took some sort of security from Jason and the others and let them go, after which the brothers sent Paul and Silas off to Berea by night (Acts 17:5–10).

The kind of assurance spoken of here is a kind of knowledge—and knowledge is a gift.

> The fear of the Lord is the beginning of knowledge: But fools despise wisdom and instruction. (Prov. 1:7)

> For that they hated knowledge, and did not choose the fear of the Lord. (Prov. 1:29)

> The fear of the Lord is the beginning of wisdom: and the knowledge of the holy is understanding. (Prov. 9:10)

The first stair step of knowing anything rightly is to know God rightly, and to fear Him. To hate knowledge is the same thing as not choosing the fear of the Lord. And knowledge of the holy is the foundation of all understanding.

Our knowledge of things is not *our* attainment. A baby is born knowing how to suck—did *he* figure that out? Knowledge is a *grace*. And Proverbs shows that knowledge is also a moral activity, and denial of given knowledge an immoral one.

When the gospel comes in power, it brings *much* assurance (v. 5). But it is also true that when the gospel comes in power it disrupts the status quo—and if there is one thing we know about the status quo, it is how much it dislikes being disrupted. The status quo *hates* that.

Philosophers call one branch of their discipline epistemology. This is the branch of philosophy that seeks to answer the question of how we know what we know, and then, how do we know that we know *that*? For philosophers it is a matter of figuring out an intellectual problem—which is a big part of their problem. To say it again, knowledge is a grace. It is a gift. Knowledge is the kindness of God. Knowledge is not something we attain; knowledge is bestowed. Given how the Almighty is going to judge us at the last day, we need to come to grips with the fact that we all know more than we think we do.

Remember how the church at Thessalonica was planted. Paul came to town and preached the gospel for three successive sabbaths. And what was accomplished in the course of those three weeks? They were delivered from the wrath to come. The Thessalonians *received* the word, with *much* assurance, in the *midst* of much affliction.

A biblical epistemology has little or nothing to do with sitting quietly in a library somewhere, thinking great and lofty thoughts, with lots of time for calm reflection. Paul did reason from the Scriptures with the Thessalonians; there was study and research involved (Acts 17:2). But then there came a time—and it was a very, very brief time—when he rolled up the scroll and asked them what they thought of Christ. Did the Christ have to suffer and rise? And this Jesus of Nazareth: was He this Christ?

The train is leaving now, and if you stay here the wrath of God remains on you (John 3:36). Today if you hear His voice, do not harden your hearts. And so, friend, what do we make of this Christ?

1 THESSALONIANS 2

TRUE MINISTRY

In the second chapter of this epistle, the apostle Paul reminds the Thessalonians of how the gospel was first brought to them. Again, we know that Paul was only there for three successive sabbaths, and so we can see here just how much authenticity in ministry can be effectively communicated within a short space of time.

> For yourselves, brethren, know our entrance in unto you, that it was not in vain: But even after that we had suffered before, and were shamefully entreated, as ye know, at Philippi, we were bold in our God to speak unto you the gospel of God with much contention. For our exhortation was not of deceit, nor of uncleanness,

> nor in guile: But as we were allowed of God to be put in trust with the gospel, even so we speak; not as pleasing men, but God, which trieth our hearts. For neither at any time used we flattering words, as ye know, nor a cloke of covetousness; God is witness: Nor of men sought we glory, neither of you, nor yet of others, when we might have been burdensome, as the apostles of Christ. But we were gentle among you, even as a nurse cherisheth her children: So being affectionately desirous of you, we were willing to have imparted unto you, not the gospel of God only, but also our own souls, because ye were dear unto us. For ye remember, brethren, our labour and travail: for labouring night and day, because we would not be chargeable unto any of you, we preached unto you the gospel of God. Ye are witnesses, and God also, how holily and justly and unblameably we behaved ourselves among you that believe: As ye know how we exhorted and comforted and charged every one of you, as a father doth his children, That ye would walk worthy of God, who hath called you unto his kingdom and glory. (1 Thess. 2:1–12)

Paul begins this second chapter by reminding the Thessalonians how Paul and his companions had first arrived in their city, and how it was not a vain entrance (v. 1). Even though they had been shamefully treated at Philippi (Acts 16), and even though there was much turmoil in Thessalonica, they were not hesitant (v. 2).

Paul then moves into a description of his ministry approach, which is a paradigm for true ministry. Paul and his helpers were not deceitful, they were not unclean, they were not tricksy (v. 3). Since God had entrusted them with the gospel, they spoke as men who needed to please the God who sees the hearts of all men (v. 4). Paul then swears here—as God is witness—they did not *flatter*, and they did not use ministry as a blanket to hide or cover up their greed (v. 5). Although as an apostle he could have set up an expense account, he and his companions did not. They did not seek to be a burden, and they did not seek glory—whether from the Thessalonians, or from any others (v. 6). Rather, they were gentle with the Thessalonians, the way a nursing mother is (v. 7). Because the Thessalonians were dear to them, they sought to impart the gospel, along with their own souls (v. 8). He reminds the Thessalonians how they labored night and day in order to avoid being a financial burden, and in order to be able to preach the gospel for free (v. 9). You are witnesses, Paul says, and then he swears again—God is also witness—just how holy, just, and blameless they had been (v. 10). The Thessalonians knew how much like a father Paul's band had been in exhorting, and comforting, and charging (v. 11). The goal was for the Thessalonians to learn to walk worthy of God, the same God who called them into His kingdom and glory (v. 12).

When ministries go astray, it is very common for the problem to be located in one of three areas: glory, gold, and girls. And because sins are like grapes—they come in bunches—it is not unusual to find some ministries that shipwreck because of all three. Paul, when recounting the blameless nature of his ministry among the Thessalonians, touches on all three points.

First, we see that Paul says "nor of men sought we *glory*" (v. 6). Second, he says (repeatedly) that he and his companions did not have a cloak "of *covetousness*" (v. 5). They were not *financially* burdensome (v. 6). They labored night and day to prevent the *expenses* from falling on the Thessalonians (v. 9). They were not after gold. And third, Paul says that their appeal did not make room for "uncleanness" (v. 3). He uses this word in a sexual sense a little bit later in the epistle (1 Thess. 4:7), and his use is overwhelmingly a reference to sexual sin in other places (Rom. 1:24; 2 Cor. 12:2; Gal. 5:19; Eph 4:19; Eph. 5:3; Col. 3:5). The ministry is not to be used as a means of impressing the girls.

The way God created us, children require *both* a father and mother. Children need tenderness, and children need toughness. We see here that the demeanors characteristic of good fathers and good mothers are supposed to be present in godly ministry.

Let's start with mothers (v. 7). The ministers and leaders in the church should be kind and gentle (*epios*) as they care for the flock. They are supposed to do this as a nursing mother (*trophos*) would behave as she cherishes (*thalpo*) her children. What we are talking about is the epitome of tenderness. (All of this is stereotyping, of course, and perfectly monstrous.)

At the same time, ministers should be fathers in the church (v. 11). You remember, Paul says, how we behaved in your midst as fathers do with their children. The three characteristics of this kind of paternal care that Paul mentions are *exhortation, encouragement,* and *charging*. The ministry team at Thessalonica wanted the Thessalonians to be upright and courageous. They wanted the Thessalonians to stand up straight. We see later on in this letter that this is exactly what they did. Paul's pastoral care resulted in the grace of the Thessalonians walking in a worthy fashion.

Paul concludes this section by explaining the whole direction of his pastoral ministry with the Thessalonians, which lines up nicely with the direction of his pastoral ministry with all believers, as we see elsewhere in his epistles. He wants to present every man perfect or complete in Christ (Col. 1:28). He is not aiming low.

So in this place in the epistle, Paul says that God has called the Thessalonians into His kingdom and glory (having done so *entirely* by grace), and then Paul crowns this comment by saying that the Thessalonians had already been exhorted to walk worthy of God. But break this down, and reflect on the deeper meaning that *has* to be here. How is it possible to walk *worthy* of *grace*?

Doesn't grace mean that we are unworthy? Doesn't *worth* mean that it is not grace? There really is a mystery here. Jesus tells us that, after we have done everything He requires of us, we should finish by saying we are worthless servants, and only did what was required (Luke 17:10). But this same Jesus says, also of a servant who did what he should have done, "Well done, good and faithful servant" (Matt. 25:21, 23). So what is it to be *worthy* in the light of God's *grace*? It is to know that you are not worthy, and in that knowledge, by faith alone, to stand up straight. You are standing in the grace that is Christ, so stand up straight.

Here is the paradox in a nutshell: "Let us therefore come *boldly* unto the throne of *grace*, that we may obtain *mercy*, and find *grace* to help in time of need" (Heb. 4:16).

What do we need? We need mercy and grace. Where do we come? We come to the throne of grace. How do we come? Not cravenly, not crawling on all fours—we come boldly.

Unforgiven, we are all tied up. And this is a knot that no sinful man can untie. The only one who could untie it is Jesus Christ, which He has done, and He is the only reason we walk free. Forgiven, we are liberated.

HOW TO HEAR A SERMON

In the first half of this chapter, Paul has recounted for the Thessalonians the kind of character that he and his co-workers displayed while they labored in Thessalonica: what kind of men preached the gospel to them? But now he moves on to describe the authority of the gospel as preached in itself.

> For this cause also thank we God without ceasing, because, when ye received the word of God which ye heard of us, ye received it not as the word of men, but as it is in truth, the word of God, which effectually worketh also in you that believe. For ye, brethren, became followers of the churches of God which in Judaea are in Christ Jesus: for ye also have suffered like things of your own countrymen, even as they have of the Jews: Who both killed the Lord Jesus, and their own prophets, and have persecuted us; and they please not God, and are contrary to all men: Forbidding us to speak to the Gentiles that they might be saved, to fill up their sins alway: for the wrath is come upon them to the uttermost.

> But we, brethren, being taken from you for a short time in presence, not in heart, endeavoured the more abundantly to see your face with great desire. Wherefore we would have come unto you, even I Paul, once and again; but Satan hindered us. For what is our hope, or joy, or crown of rejoicing? Are not even ye in the presence of our Lord Jesus Christ at his coming? For ye are our glory and joy. (1 Thess. 2:13–20)

Paul says that he constantly thanks God for the reception that the Thessalonians gave to the preached message (v. 13). When they first heard Paul's preaching, they received it, not as a word from men, but as it was in fact, the Word of God. As the Word of God, it worked powerfully in the lives of those who believed it (v. 13). The Thessalonians became, in effect, the younger brothers of the believers in Judea. The Judean believers had been persecuted by their countrymen, and then the same thing happened to the Thessalonians (v. 14). The Jews had murdered the Lord Jesus and their own prophets, and they were persecuting the apostles. They displeased God, and they were contrary to all men (v. 15). They were getting in the way of those preaching to the Gentiles, and this is why utmost wrath was coming down on them (v. 16). This *utmost wrath* likely refers to the impending judgment that was about to fall on Jerusalem in AD 70. We should be careful to dispatch any antisemitic sentiments that some might want to assign to this kind of statement. It is true that the Jews did these awful things to Christ and the apostles. It is also true that Paul makes the point of saying that the

Thessalonians got exactly the same treatment from *their* unregenerate countrymen. This viciousness is not how Jews are; it is how unregenerate *people* are.

Paul had to leave the Thessalonians for a brief time, and longed greatly to see them again (v. 17). He attempted to revisit them repeatedly, but Satan hindered those efforts (v. 18). What is Paul's reward? What is his hope, joy, or crown of rejoicing? (v. 19). Paul's reward is seeing the Thessalonians stand in the presence of Christ at His coming (v. 19). *They* are Paul's glory and joy (v. 20).

We learn in this place how to hear a sermon. Paul says that when he and his group first arrived in Thessalonica, they preached the gospel. He goes on to commend the Thessalonians for how they listened. They received the message proclaimed, not as the words of men, but as the Word of God Himself. God speaks in and through the gospel.

The Scriptures *are* the Word of God. When you open your Bible, you don't have to hunt around in order to try to find something God said. He said it all. There is a theological school of thought (neo-orthodoxy) that teaches that the Bible is the place where you might *encounter* or meet with the Word of God—and then again, maybe not. This is obviously a deficient view, but we can take an illustration from it. This is not how to approach the Bible, but it can be a helpful way to approach a *sermon*.

When a minister of the Word, lawfully called and set apart, stands before you with an open Bible in order to expound what it says, you should prepare your hearts to encounter the Word of God. You should come to worship expecting *Christ* to speak to you. Evangelical sermons are not the Bible, stem to stern. Obviously not. But *something* happens there, and when it happens, it is a profound work of the Spirit.

> If any man speak, *let him speak as the oracles of God*. (1 Pet. 4:11)

> How then shall they call on him in whom they have not believed? and how shall they believe in him of *whom* they have not heard? and how shall they hear without a preacher? (Rom. 10:14)

In this Romans passage, there is a translation issue. Without getting into the weeds, the verb (*akouo*) takes a different case ending for the object than verbs usually do. This makes the difference between *whom* and *of whom*. When you listen to the gospel preached, are you hearing *about* Jesus, or are you hearing Jesus? How can men believe in the one *whom* they have not heard?

So when the sermon accords with the text, and the people are listening in faith, then and there, in that place, Jesus Christ is speaking to His people. The Second Helvetic Confession puts it this way: "The preaching of the Word of God is the Word of God" (Ch. 1). And J.I. Packer says this:

> The true idea of preaching is that the preacher should become a mouthpiece for his text, opening it up and applying it as a word from God to his hearers, talking only in order that the text may speak itself and be heard, making each point from his text in such a manner 'that

the hearers may discern how God teacheth it from hence' (Westminster Directory, 1645).[1]

The proclamation of the gospel offers a personal encounter with God. The Scriptures are not embarrassed to promise us staggering rewards in the next life for faithfulness in this life. The promise of reward has been mocked by some ("opiate of the masses") and thoughtlessly pursued by others, as if God were going to give them a chest full of gold doubloons for having been such good boys. Now the fact of the promised rewards is undeniable, but we also have to consider the *nature* of the rewards. They are all bound up in personal relationships. Paul says that his crown is made up of Thessalonians. They were his hope, joy, and crown of rejoicing. *They* were his glory and joy. This is more like a wedding day than a pay day. The *relationship* is the reward.

Consider how this flows out from what was said just before. When the gospel is preached in power, Christ Himself meets with His people. And when Christ meets with His people, His people also meet with His people (1 John 1:7). This is how fellowship in the Spirit arises. One Lord, one faith, one baptism. One body, one Spirit.

Sermons are not sacraments, but I think it is fair to say that they are sacramentals. A sermon is not a lecture, or a talk. It is not a chat about the things of God. It is a declaration. But unless Christ picks it up and uses it for His intended purposes, a sermon makes the hollowest sound any mortal has ever heard. Christ speaks with authority, and not as the

---

1. J.I. Packer, *God Has Spoken* (Downers Grove, IL: InterVarsity Press, 1979), 28.

scribes (Matt. 7:29). But He has so much authority that He can even pick up a scribe and do wonderful things through him. Every mortal preacher is in this position, and needs to keep it in mind at all times. Remember how Paul once cried out in a holy despair: "Who is sufficient for these things?" (2 Cor. 2:6). The best preacher in the world is nothing more than a fifteen-dollar yard sale violin. But when Christ picks that thing up, He still astonishes the world with the music He can make.

Christ is the revelation of God Himself, and He cannot be other than what He is. He is the revelation. He is the manifold grace of God. When He is preached, there *He* is made manifest. Christ is present. How could He not be? He is the Word of God.

1 THESSALONIANS 3

THE MINES OF DIFFICULTY

The second stanza of an old Isaac Watts hymn asks a quite reasonable question. It is a question that we—accustomed as we are to so many creature comforts—should be willing to ask ourselves more often than we do.

> Must I be carried to the skies
>   On flowery beds of ease,
> While others fought to win the prize
>   And sailed through bloody seas?

The faithful Christian life is not one that can be characterized as reclining on "flowery beds of ease."

> Wherefore when we could no longer forbear, we thought it good to be left at Athens alone; And sent Timotheus, our brother, and minister of God, and our fellowlabourer in the gospel of Christ, to establish you, and to comfort you concerning your faith: That no man should be moved by these afflictions: for yourselves know that we are appointed thereunto. For verily, when we were with you, we told you before that we should suffer tribulation; even as it came to pass, and ye know. For this cause, when I could no longer forbear, I sent to know your faith, lest by some means the tempter have tempted you, and our labour be in vain. (1 Thess. 3:1–5)

After mentioning again how dear the Thessalonians were to him, Paul goes on to say that when he couldn't stand it anymore, he thought it best for him to be left in Athens alone (v. 1), and he commissioned Timothy to go back to Thessalonica in order to establish and comfort them (v. 2). This was a significant move because Timothy was important to Paul also. Timothy was Paul's brother and fellow-worker, as well as a minister and servant of God (v. 2). It was a sacrifice for Paul to send him. Now the reason for sending Timothy was because the Thessalonians were going through afflictions at the hands of their own countrymen (as mentioned in the previous chapter), and Paul wanted to ensure that they were taught well enough when it came to such afflictions. He didn't want any man to be moved or unsettled or surprised by them (v. 3a), and he wanted to remind the Thessalonians that as believers we are *appointed* to them

(v. 3b). Paul had predicted all of it beforehand, when he was still in Thessalonica. He had told them what was going to happen (v. 4).

And the Thessalonians had seen it come to pass with their own eyes. That was the reason why Paul was beside himself with concern. So he sent Timothy to them to find out if the tempter had followed up the affliction with temptation, in such a way as to unwind all of Paul's labors there (v. 5). Notice that there are two elements here that Paul is concerned about. The first is the trial itself, and the second is the devil's interpretation of it. Having a toothache is bad enough, but the suggestion that it is happening because God hates you is much worse. The deeper concern is the second one, the spin the devil puts on any trial.

We need to remember the unbelievers' intentions for believers. In the previous chapter, Paul reminded the Thessalonians that the Jews in Judea were "contrary to all men." They were full of malice and hostility. They did not want Gentiles to be saved. They had murdered the Lord Jesus. They had killed their own prophets. They had persecuted the apostles. Paul knew the heart of man, and he knew the inevitable reaction whenever renewed hearts come into contact with unregenerate hearts. There is nothing you can do that will prevent this reaction from happening. It happened to Jesus Himself, and it has been happening to His followers ever since.

The thing you *can* do is prepare—you can teach Christians what to expect. Far too many Christians think a negative reaction is the result of them being a poor testimony. We have gotten to the point where we define vile behavior as any behavior that provokes someone else into behaving in a vile fashion. We look at rioters and blame the people who never riot.

The idea that Christians can draw a negative reaction because they have had such a *good* testimony scarcely occurs to us. Did Jesus have a poor testimony? Is that why *He* was killed?

So what is God's intention for believers? God governs everything, and this means that God must have a purpose for us in our afflictions. What is He up to? Our adversaries have one thing in mind, but does God have a contrary purpose in mind with regard to this kind of situation?

> And when they had preached the gospel to that city, and had taught many, they returned again to Lystra, and to Iconium, and Antioch, confirming the souls of the disciples, and exhorting them to continue in the faith, *and that we must through much tribulation enter into the kingdom of God.* (Acts 14:21–22)

> And not only so, but *we glory in tribulations also*: knowing that tribulation worketh patience; And patience, experience; and experience, hope: And hope maketh not ashamed; because the love of God is shed abroad in our hearts by the Holy Ghost which is given unto us. (Rom. 5:3–5)

We glory in tribulations, not because we are masochistic, but because we know that the rocky pathway winds up to the great mountaintop city. Still, we sometimes look at the immediate landscape, which can be pretty grim, instead of looking at what is really happening. We look at how hard the path *is*, instead of where the hard path *goes*.

What is really happening is that God is using the process to fit us for our final destination. The hard path prepares us for the glory to be found at the end of the road. There is a fitting suitability between our trials now and our glory then. What is this difficulty that we must go through? Look at it with the eyes that Paul wanted the Thessalonians to have. Your difficulties are the love of God, shed abroad in your heart.

We have considered the intentions of the unbelievers and the intentions of God in our trials. What should be our own intentions? We must learn wisdom. This means we must *reject* the purpose that unbelievers have for our afflictions, and yet we must also *embrace* the purpose that God has for those same afflictions. We know that God does not tempt any man (James 1:13), but we also know that the Spirit led Jesus into the wilderness to be tempted (Matt. 4:1). What's more, we are instructed to pray for God to lead us not into temptation (Matt. 6:13). This is not a contradiction. The same event can be both a *trial* and a *temptation*; the same Greek word is used for both. The difficult event that is assigned to us by God—"to which we were appointed"—is an event that has different intentions on either side of it. God uses it to *strengthen* you, and the devil wants to use it to *weaken* you.

So we must learn to walk straight, which means that we must first learn to *think* straight. The way into the kingdom of God is fraught with difficulty. But this does not mean that just because something is difficult, it must be the way into the kingdom. Remember that wrath was coming upon the unbelieving Jews "to the uttermost." The destruction of Jerusalem was difficult, but that is the *only* thing that it was. As Proverbs says, "Good understanding giveth favour: But the way of transgressors is hard" (Prov. 13:15).

So the diamonds of the promise can only be found in the mines of difficulty—and some of those mines go very deep. But there are other mine shafts that are filled with nothing but useless rocks, and many thousands have spent their lives down in those holes.

What then is the difference? The difference is Christ, and the pursuit of Christ.

The check on our hearts should be this: Are we pursuing Christ and His kingdom? Is that what we want? Is that what we want regardless? Is that what we want above all else? Then the diamonds are most certainly there. Seek first His kingdom.

FACE TO FACE

This first letter to the Thessalonians was inspired by the Holy Spirit, and is a portion of the Word of God. But at the same time, it was Paul's second choice. What he really wanted was to be together with the Thessalonians, face to face, so that he could truly encourage them.

> But now when Timotheus came from you unto us, and brought us good tidings of your faith and charity, and that ye have good remembrance of us always, desiring

greatly to see us, as we also to see you: Therefore, brethren, we were comforted over you in all our affliction and distress by your faith: For now we live, if ye stand fast in the Lord. For what thanks can we render to God again for you, for all the joy wherewith we joy for your sakes before our God; Night and day praying exceedingly that we might see your face, and might perfect that which is lacking in your faith?

Now God himself and our Father, and our Lord Jesus Christ, direct our way unto you. And the Lord make you to increase and abound in love one toward another, and toward all men, even as we do toward you: To the end he may stablish your hearts unblameable in holiness before God, even our Father, at the coming of our Lord Jesus Christ with all his saints. (1 Thess. 3:6–13)

Remember that Paul had said earlier that he was beside himself with concern over how the Thessalonians were doing, which is why he sent Timothy to them (1 Thess. 3:1-5). Now he says that Timothy had returned to him with very good news: the Thessalonians' faith and love were solid, and they had fond memories of Paul (v. 6). They wanted to see Paul and company, and the feeling went both ways. That news was a comfort to Paul in the middle of his afflictions and distress.

It was such good news that Paul describes it in terms of life: "for now we live" (v. 8). It was like a resurrection. The Thessalonians standing fast was life to Paul. Paul had so much joy over them that he was without words when it came to rendering thanks to God (v. 9). Paul had been praying day and night, and doing so "exceedingly," as he asked for two things. First, he wanted to see the Thessalonians face to face, and second, he wanted to be able to complete or perfect whatever was lacking in their faith (v. 10). And so he repeats his prayer request again—that God Himself, the Father, and the Lord Jesus Christ "direct our way unto you" (v. 11). He also prays that God would make the Thessalonians grow and increase in their love for one another, not to mention for everyone else, in the same way that Paul feels about them (v. 12). The purpose of this is so that their hearts might be established without blame in holiness before God the Father, until the *parousia* of the Lord Jesus with all His saints (v. 13).

One of the challenges we will have as we work through the two letters to the Thessalonians is the challenge of distinguishing the end of the age (which occurred in AD 70) from the end of the world (which will occur we know not when). I am taking the reference to the *parousia* at the end of our text here as referring to the destruction of Jerusalem, and the passage coming up in 1 Thessalonians 4:16 as referring to the Final Coming.

The word *parousia* simply means arrival, coming, or presence. The word is *not* a synonym for the Second Coming. Paul uses it for his own arrival (2 Cor. 10:10; Phil. 1:26; 2:12), and for the arrival of his companions (1 Cor 16:17; 2 Cor. 7:6–7). He even uses it to refer to the arrival of the man of lawlessness (2 Thess. 2:9). And there are also (obviously) references to the coming of Jesus, as in our text here (1 Thess. 3:13). There is no *a priori* reason why the word might not refer to different kinds of "arrivals" or manifestations of the Lord's presence or power. So I take this as a coming in judgment on Jerusalem, the appearance of the Lord being manifested in the complete fulfillment of His prophecy that Jerusalem was not going to have one stone left on another. The phrasing is likely an allusion to Zechariah: "And ye shall flee to the valley of the mountains; For the valley of the mountains shall reach unto Azal: Yea, ye shall flee, like as ye fled from before the earthquake in the days of Uzziah king of Judah: And *the Lord my God shall come, and all the saints with thee*" (Zech. 14:5).

Here are the reasons for thinking that we are talking about a visitation of wrath in the first century. The first chapter refers to the "wrath to come" (1 Thess. 1:10). The Jews in chapter two fight against Gentiles receiving the gospel, and Paul says that "wrath is come upon them to the uttermost" (1 Thess. 2:16). This is clearly a reference to AD 70. What's more, this letter was written circa AD 50/51, and during Passover in AD 49, there had been a massacre of thousands of Jews at the Temple. Also the emperor Claudius had expelled all Jews from Rome in that same year. Such events were not the fullness of wrath, but the pot was certainly starting to shake, and Paul was clearly expecting it to boil all over the stove. Although he moves on to talk about the end of the world in chapter four, we make *that* determination from the immediate context found in that place ("the dead in Christ shall rise"). But from the descriptions in the first three chapters, we have no reason to believe that Paul has moved out of the first century yet.

Surprisingly enough, the last portion of this passage also has some lessons for us on distance learning. Notice how deeply Paul yearns for the growth of the Thessalonians in holiness. Also notice that he "settles" for writing to them. He would much prefer to see them face to face. He prayed exceedingly that he might be able to see them in person.

Catechized by our digital world, we think we have conquered distance when we really haven't. Our letters have gotten much more sophisticated than they were in Paul's day, but our "face-to-face" communication is not really the equivalent of being there. Our texting, and Zoom meetings, and online sermons, and POD books, and blogs, and phone calls, are just souped-up letters. They are not an adequate replacement for in-person community. Paul would have used them all, but he still would have yearned to be with the Thessalonians, in the same room, breathing the same air, and not through a mask either.

As we grow in the Lord, notice that it is the Lord who enables us to grow in the Lord. God gives the increase. When we increase and abound in love for one another, this is not our doing. It is being done within us, but also *for* us. The Lord is the one who makes us love each other, and He is the one who establishes us in holiness. Love for Christ is part of the work of Christ. We are commanded to love Him, and this command to bear fruit is fulfilled as the fruit of the Spirit.

Notice this from verse 12: Paul's prayer is that *God* would enable the Thessalonians to grow. As we are talking about life, it is God who must give the increase. The great Augustine once put it this way: "Give what you command, and command what you will."

1 THESSALONIANS 4

NOT LIKE THE GENTILES

We come now to the passage in Thessalonians that addresses the vast difference between the Christian sexual ethic and a pagan sexual ethic. We want to be careful here because there is a ditch on both sides of the road. (There is always a ditch on both sides of the road.) Some Christians have confused being fastidious with being holy, and those two things are not the same thing at all. Other Christians have veered off the road on the opposite side, and are currently drinking all the ditch water that the porn industry can supply. So let us try to stay on the road, shall we?

> Furthermore then we beseech you, brethren, and exhort you by the Lord Jesus, that as ye have received

of us how ye ought to walk and to please God, so ye would abound more and more. For ye know what commandments we gave you by the Lord Jesus. For this is the will of God, even your sanctification, that ye should abstain from fornication: That every one of you should know how to possess his vessel in sanctification and honour; Not in the lust of concupiscence, even as the Gentiles which know not God: That no man go beyond and defraud his brother in any matter: because that the Lord is the avenger of all such, as we also have forewarned you and testified. For God hath not called us unto uncleanness, but unto holiness. He therefore that despiseth, despiseth not man, but God, who hath also given unto us his holy Spirit. (1 Thess. 4:1–8)

We have seen how dear the Thessalonians were to Paul, and these exhortations are built on that foundation (v. 1). Because the Thessalonians had received Paul's teaching on how to please God, he now begs them to do this *more and more* (v. 1). "For you know," he says, "what commandments we gave you by the Lord Jesus" (v. 2). Sanctification is God's will for them, especially sexual sanctification (v. 3). Everyone should know how to "possess his vessel" in sanctification and honor (v. 4). This is contrasted with the "lust of concupiscence," which is characteristic of Gentiles who do not know God (v. 5). Sexual immorality is not victimless. Paul says here that it is a matter of *defrauding* your brother—and *God* is the avenger for the defrauded one (v. 6). In addition, Paul says that sin in this area is "going beyond," as in trespassing. God's calling for us is not to uncleanness, but rather to holiness (v. 7). If a man despises this commandment, he is not primarily despising man, but rather God (v. 8)—the same God who has given us His Holy Spirit. Sexual sin is therefore sin against *God*. When David confessed his sin of adultery and murder, he turned to God saying, "Against thee, thee only, have I sinned" (Ps. 51:4). Our sins entail other people, and harm them, but the law that is broken is God's.

Far too many Christians, particularly in our own Reformed camp, think of their Christian lives as having the ultimate goal of somehow "not displeasing" God. Like the servant in the parable, they think their master is a hard master, and so their objective is simply to stay out of trouble. And that's actually how they get into trouble. We have to realize that there is actually a real prospect of living in such a way as to please God.

Notice that Paul had taught the Thessalonians how to walk in a way that *pleased God*, and now he wants them to do this *more and more*. Holiness is not the absence of sin, although cleansing from sin is a precondition for that holiness. Kingdom holiness is righteousness, peace, and joy in the Holy Spirit (Rom. 14:17). It is the *presence* of something, and it is crowned with the pleasure of God. What's more, there is always room for advancement in that pleasure and in that joy.

This is also a good place for us to note that the phrase "the will of God" has to be understood in two senses. Here is the question: can the will of God ever be thwarted? The answer to that is both "certainly not" and "of course." The *decretive* will of God cannot be thwarted by anyone at any time. Even

Nebuchadnezzar knew this (Dan. 4:35). If God has determined that something will happen, then that something is *going* to happen. If He has decreed that it not happen, it is not going to happen.

God's *preceptive* will has to do with what He has commanded us to do. This will *can* be thwarted, which is why we are instructed in verse 3 not to disobey that will. We are told not to disobey God's preceptive will because it is possible that we *could* disobey it.

And remember there are also times when the two kinds of wills intersect. When Jesus died on the cross, it was the will of God (Luke 22:42; Acts 4:26–28) even though it was accomplished by wicked hands (Acts 2:23). The violation of God's *preceptive* will by Judas, Herod, Pontius Pilate, and the Sanhedrin was the instrument God used to accomplish His *decretive* will. We must always remember that God is God, and we are not.

So we then come to the question of "possessing your own vessel." What is that?

There is an ambiguity here. When Paul says that each one should know how to "possess his vessel," is he talking about the person's own body, or is he talking about that man's wife? It is true either way, and it amounts to the same kind of behavior either way, but I am taking it in the latter sense. In brief, my reason for doing this is that the immediate antecedent is the fact that God's will is for us to abstain from fornication, and it is followed by a rejection of the "lust of concupiscence," both of which appear to have other people involved. But in either case, it all comes down to a man's self-control.

When it comes to sexual behavior, it is not a contrast between the Gentiles *possessing* and the Christians *not possessing*. Both possess "their vessels." But unbelievers do so with dishonor, uncleanness, passionate lust, fraudulence, and contempt. Don't possess anything *that* way, Paul says.

By way of contrast, he requires sexual behavior from Christians (not sexless behavior) that is sanctified, honorable, honest, clean, and holy. When Paul says in 1 Corinthians that our bodies are temples of the Holy Spirit, he is talking about avoiding sexual impurity (1 Cor. 6:18). All other sins a man commits are outside the body, but he who sins sexually is defiling that temple. Paul was not talking about how you all need to go to the gym more, although you might, or how you must avoid refined sugar or transfats. (Something is transfat, for example, when a baby carrot identifies as salty grease on the inside.)

The Thessalonians had learned from Paul how they were supposed to behave in this area (vv. 1-2). He *taught* on it. To leave the subject untouched (for the sake of remaining prissy and fastidious, as mentioned earlier) will not leave our children in some neutral zone. *It will not protect them*. The world does not hesitate to catechize everyone in their sexual mores—through sex ed, through pop entertainment, and through porn. But in our revolt against this, we want to be joyful in holiness, not grim in our moralism.

And this brings us to the question of justification and the pleasure of God. We are called to live in such a way as to please God. But this is not possible without the baseline of justification—the legal and forensic declaration of *not guilty* in the court chambers of Heaven. Our free and complete justification sets us free to pursue our sanctification without timidity.

Because of that great declaration of *not guilty*, we have *no condemnation* (Rom. 8:1). On the foundation of that great declaration, we are set free to be spiritually minded, which is life and peace (Rom. 8:6). To fall short of this, to be carnally minded, results in what? It means that those who are in the flesh *cannot please God* (Rom. 8:8).

And this is why we declare Christ as our righteousness, as our complete justification. Because of that, and only because of that, His Spirit is at work in our lives for our sanctification, which includes our sexual lives—whether in thought, words, or deeds.

EARTHLY GOOD AND THE HEAVENLY MIND

In the next portion of this letter, we find a marvelous balance between our daily mundane concerns and our ultimate eschatological concerns. A taunt is sometimes leveled against certain Christians that they are "so heavenly-minded that they are no earthly good." But this is not how it works, actually.

C.S. Lewis summed the situation up nicely when he said this:

> If you read history you will find that the Christians who did most for the present world were just those who thought most of the next. . . . It is since Christians have largely ceased to think of the other world that they have become so ineffective in this. Aim at Heaven

and you will get earth 'thrown in': aim at earth and you will get neither."[2]

With that in mind, consider the words of the apostle.

> But as touching brotherly love ye need not that I write unto you: for ye yourselves are taught of God to love one another. And indeed ye do it toward all the brethren which are in all Macedonia: but we beseech you, brethren, that ye increase more and more; And that ye study to be quiet, and to do your own business, and to work with your own hands, as we commanded you; That ye may walk honestly toward them that are without, and that ye may have lack of nothing.
>
> But I would not have you to be ignorant, brethren, concerning them which are asleep, that ye sorrow not, even as others which have no hope. For if we believe that Jesus died and rose again, even so them also which sleep in Jesus will God bring with him. For this we say unto you by the word of the Lord, that we which are alive and remain unto the coming of the Lord shall not prevent them which are asleep. For the Lord himself shall descend from heaven with a shout, with the voice of the archangel, and with the trump of God: and the dead in Christ shall rise first: Then we which are alive and remain shall be caught up together with them in the clouds, to meet the Lord in the air: and so shall we

---

1. C.S. Lewis, *Mere Christianity* (New York: HarperOne, 1980), 134.

ever be with the Lord. Wherefore comfort one another with these words. (1 Thess. 4:9–18)

Paul begins by saying that he does not need to teach the Thessalonians about brotherly love—for God Himself had taught them about that (v. 9). They were practicing what they had been taught to do, loving all the brothers throughout Macedonia (v. 10). Again, Paul's plea is that they do what they already knew how to do, but to do so *more and more* (v. 10). However, this active love is not to be understood as a busybody love. It studies to be quiet (v. 11), to mind its own business (v. 11), and to work with its own hands (v. 11), as Paul had commanded. The reason for this ethic is so that the Thessalonians could walk honestly before outsiders, not lacking anything (v. 12).

Paul does not want the Thessalonians to be in the dark over what happens to fellow believers who "fall asleep in the Lord" (v. 13). They should not sorrow over them in the same way as those who have no hope (v. 13). For if Jesus died and rose, even so those who have fallen asleep will be brought back to earth by God when Christ returns (v. 14). For Paul assures them by the word of the Lord that those who survive to the Lord's appearing will have no advantage over those who have died beforehand (v. 15). The Lord will descend from Heaven with a shout, an archangel's voice, and the trumpet of God, and the dead in Christ will be the first to rise (v. 16). Those alive at that time will follow after (v. 17). These are to be words of comfort (v. 18).

Now the great Pauline principle here is "mind thine own business." Tend to thine own knitting. You do this, *not* because you are telling the rest of the body to get lost, but rather because you need to acquire something before you can give it. You cannot give what you do not have, and you cannot have something to give unless you came by it honestly. Paul says something very close to this in Ephesians, when he tells the thief to work with his hands instead of pilfering with them. The reason is so that he might have something to *give* (Eph. 4:28). Loving more and more means gathering more and more, which means minding the store, and then being generous with what you have gained.

We give in order to get, in order that we might be able to give even more. When it comes to good works, you need to maintain a positive cash flow—which means you can't be a good works miser, and you can't be a good works spendthrift.

Notice how this works. Paul tells the Thessalonians that they were already loving the brothers throughout all of Macedonia, and he urges them on. Do this *more and more*, he says. With this as the basic baseline charge, what is the action he then demands? Study to be quiet. Mind your own business. Work with your hands. Conduct your business honestly. Save your money.

And Paul says we should do all of our mundane work with the Lord's Final Coming on our minds. This is a juxtaposition that has radical implications for societal transformation. (We should keep in mind the fact that even if the End does not happen in our lifetime, which seems likely, all of us alive today are going to meet our Maker within a hundred years or so.)

As Paul moves seamlessly into his next topic, we learn that Monday morning in the workplace and the end of the world are actually all part of the same subject. He is not really changing topics. What he is teaching about the end of the world is to be used as comfort in the here and now.

In the short time that Paul and the Thessalonians had been acquainted, some of the saints in the Thessalonian church had already died. Perhaps this was the result of persecution—we don't know. There was therefore some concern among the Thessalonians that these departed saints were somehow going to "miss out" if the Lord came. What was going to happen to them? Paul says that the benefit actually goes the opposite way. When the Lord comes, the dead in Christ will rise first, and then those who remain alive until that glorious day will be transfigured. Then we will all be together with the Lord, and we will be with Him together forever.

As mentioned before, not every *parousia* in Scripture refers to what is popularly called the Second Coming. But *this* appearing does unmistakably refer to the end of the world. If you have any doubts, look at the events that surround it. There is a general resurrection of the dead. The living are caught up into the clouds. There is a great shout, probably that of the archangel. There is the last trumpet blast. The Lord descends from Heaven. This is *not* a description of the demolition of Jerusalem in AD 70.

The strongest argument of those who want to locate all of this within the first century is that other passages that have traditionally been applied to the end of the world turn out to have been fulfilled in the destruction of Jerusalem. If one is good, then two must be better, right? If the sun, moon, and stars are said to be shaken, and that means Jerusalem is going down, then why can't the language that this passage contains be figurative in the same way? The answer is that the Old

Testament teaches how to handle all such passages. Isaiah says that his decreation language about the solar system (Isa. 13:10) is actually an oracle against the king of Babylon (Isa. 13:1). But the Old Testament language about the resurrection is all about . . . the resurrection of the dead. After worms destroy this body, yet in my flesh shall I see God (Job 19:26).

Think of a great king coming to visit a city. The dignitaries of that city come out to meet him—but having met him, they do not all go away. No, they meet him as he comes and then escort him back into the city. This is how it will be when the Lord comes. He appears with great fanfare, the dead rise first, the living are transfigured and catch up from behind, they all meet the Lord in the air, and then return with Him to Earth. And so we will ever be with the Lord.

This is the time when Heaven and Earth kiss. This is not a loss of Heaven; it is the remarriage of Heaven and Earth. So in the work of the saints in this life (1 Cor. 15:58), we should be able to see God's declared purpose of bringing Heaven and Earth back together (Eph. 1:10). The Fall was the point where Heaven was "removed" to an almost infinite distance. But in and through Christ we are privileged to learn that Heaven is close, and by grace can be opened to us, and it is merely one short dove flight above the Jordan.

So when the Lord descends from Heaven, He will come down to your shop, your office, and your kitchen. He will come down to inspect His workmanship (Eph. 2:10), and He will look at your work as part of that (1 Tim. 6:18; Titus 2:14, 3:8, 3:14). This is because your work *is* part of His workmanship, and all of it is under a thick layer of grace, grace upon grace.

1 THESSALONIANS 5

THE DAY OF THE LORD

As we work through this next portion of Paul's letter to the Thessalonians, we want to continue to hold the various elements of "the last things" loosely, and in the palm of our hand. After we have all the pieces on the workbench before us (i.e., after 2 Thessalonians 2), we will then look at how they all relate to one another. For the moment, to help keep things clear in our minds, I am going to begin referring to the end of all things as the *Final Coming*, and not the *Second Coming*. This is to budget for the fact that Christ "comes" whenever He comes in judgment, as He did with Jerusalem in AD 70.

At the same time, we should work through all of this in real humility, remembering that Augustine, one of the greatest minds in the history of the church, once said of 2 Thessalonians 2, "I frankly confess I do not know what he means."

> But of the times and the seasons, brethren, ye have no need that I write unto you. For yourselves know perfectly that the day of the Lord so cometh as a thief in the night. For when they shall say, Peace and safety; then sudden destruction cometh upon them, as travail upon a woman with child; and they shall not escape. But ye, brethren, are not in darkness, that that day should overtake you as a thief. Ye are all the children of light, and the children of the day: we are not of the night, nor of darkness. Therefore let us not sleep, as do others; but let us watch and be sober. For they that sleep sleep in the night; and they that be drunken are drunken in the night. But let us, who are of the day, be sober, putting on the breastplate of faith and love; and for an helmet, the hope of salvation. For God hath not appointed us to wrath, but to obtain salvation by our Lord Jesus Christ, who died for us, that, whether we wake or sleep, we should live together with him. Wherefore comfort yourselves together, and edify one another, even as also ye do. (1 Thess. 5:1–11)

Paul had not had the opportunity to teach the Thessalonians everything he had wanted to, but he *had* already covered this. You know the "times and seasons," he says (v. 1). The day of the Lord will be sudden and unexpected, like a thief in the night (v. 2). (Be aware that throughout Scripture, the phrase "the day of the Lord" is commonly used for any number of historical judgments. The day of the Lord is not necessarily the Final Coming.) When the unbelievers are expecting peace and safety, they will suddenly give birth to "sudden destruction" (v. 3). Their complacency was a moral darkness, not an intellectual one (v. 4).

The believers in Thessalonica were children of the day, children of light, which would prevent the day from overtaking them like a thief (vv. 4–5). Paul's exhortation is that they *remain* awake and sober (v. 6). Sleep and drunkenness belong to the night, not to the day (v. 7). Those who are of the day should be sober, putting on the helmet of the hope of salvation, and the breastplate of faith and love (v. 8). The reason for this preventative behavior is that God has not appointed them to wrath (as He did the others), but rather to obtain salvation through Christ (v. 9). Christ died for those believers who were already dead, and for those who remained alive, so that all would be enabled to live through Him (v. 10). These were to be words of comfort and edification, which Paul assumed the Thessalonians would continue in (v. 11).

Paul obviously has the Thessalonians of the first century living in a state of high alert. They are to be awake, and with their armor on. If they could read these words of his to them, and *not* be looking out the window at what might be happening in their day, then they wouldn't be paying close attention. That tone of urgency is very clear in this passage. Just as I have argued that the presence of the general resurrection is an indication we are talking about the Final Coming, so also the presence of an "any minute now" vibe indicates that we are talking about the events that run up to the destruction of Jerusalem in AD 70. In the two letters of Thessalonians, we have both elements weaving in and out of each other.

As the first century Christians were navigating their way through a very dark pagan century, they were warned by Paul against some very real perils in *their* day. Formal emperor worship had begun under Augustus, and Thessalonica had a temple to the emperor. In AD 41, Caligula had ordered a statue of himself to be set up in the Temple at Jerusalem, which was only forestalled because Caligula was murdered (we'll cover this event in more detail later). And Nero had a bronze statue of himself built in the forecourt of one of his homes, a statue that was 120 feet tall—that's like a ten-story building.

There were certain signs that indicated the pending destruction of Jerusalem (the day of the Lord), and that destruction was something that had to occur before there could be a Final Coming. That Final Coming *was* in Paul's view, but it was like a very high and distant mountain range behind the mountain range they were about to cross.

The Jewish War would "fill up" the sins of Israel (Matt. 23:32). That event would begin the "times of the Gentiles," a period that would eventually be completed. I take that completion as being marked by the conversion of Jews, an event that has not yet happened (Rom. 11:15). This means we are still living in the times of the Gentiles.

Once the judgment starts, there is no time to *begin* to prepare. The judgment might be temporal and historical (a day of the Lord), or it might be the Final Coming. And the "final things" can overtake any of us at any time, as had already happened with some of the Thessalonians. In any case, the daylight is coming, and so Paul's charge to us is to act as though the day has already come. We are not to be ethically groggy. You don't want to be among those who were appointed to wrath—because *that* appointment will be kept. Rather, we should yearn to be among those who will "obtain salvation by our Lord Jesus Christ, who died for us" (v. 9–10).

And this brings us back to the everlasting center—Christ, our Lord. Because He was not overcome by the night, it becomes possible for all those who have trusted in Him to follow Him and to do the same.

A CLUSTER OF EXHORTATIONS

Virtues and vices are like grapes—they come in clusters. Paul is following his usual pattern here, which is to conclude his letter with a burst of ethical exhortations, all of which should be arranged within the larger framework of what he has established earlier in the letter.

> And we beseech you, brethren, to know them which labour among you, and are over you in the Lord, and admonish you; And to esteem them very highly in love for their work's sake. And be at peace among yourselves. Now we exhort you, brethren, warn them that are unruly, comfort the feebleminded, support the weak, be patient toward all men. See that none render evil for evil unto any man; but ever follow that which is good, both among yourselves, and to all men.

Rejoice evermore. Pray without ceasing. In every thing give thanks: for this is the will of God in Christ Jesus concerning you. Quench not the Spirit. Despise not prophesyings. Prove all things; hold fast that which is good. Abstain from all appearance of evil.

And the very God of peace sanctify you wholly; and I pray God your whole spirit and soul and body be preserved blameless unto the coming of our Lord Jesus Christ. Faithful is he that calleth you, who also will do it.

Brethren, pray for us. Greet all the brethren with an holy kiss.

I charge you by the Lord that this epistle be read unto all the holy brethren.

The grace of our Lord Jesus Christ be with you. Amen. (1 Thess. 5:12–28)

So the letter to the Thessalonians concludes with a cluster of rapid-fire exhortations: "Remember this, and also that, and then here is something else." The first thing Paul reminds them of is their duty to the leaders of their church. *Know* those who labor, who rule, and who admonish (v. 12). Paul says to esteem them highly, and to be at peace (v. 13). And being at peace with one another is actually a good way to esteem them.

In the next verse, he says to be hard and to be soft, depending on who you are dealing with (v. 14). Hard all the time is no good, and neither is soft all the time. Don't be the kind of person who retaliates, whether inside the church or outside (v. 15). Rejoice all the time, in every circumstance (v. 16). Pray without ceasing (v. 17). Give thanks in every situation (v. 18). Don't quench the Spirit (v. 19). Don't treat prophecy with contempt (v. 20). Test everything, and cling to what passes the test (v. 21). Abstain from every form of evil (v. 22). Do these things and God will preserve you till the coming of Christ. He is faithful and *He* will do it (vv. 23–24). Paul then requests prayer for his work (v. 25). Greet one another with a kiss (v. 26). The letter is to be read to all (v. 27). And may the grace of Christ with be you (v. 28). And amen.

There are a number of places where we quietly assume that certain practices are human traditions when they are actually profoundly biblical. One of those things is the biblical practice of church membership. We think that membership is a human invention when it is actually a scriptural requirement. Set vv. 12–13 here in this passage alongside Hebrews 13:7 and 13:17 and see what happens.

> Remember them which have the rule over you, who have spoken unto you the word of God: whose faith follow, considering the end of their conversation. (Heb. 13:7)

> Obey them that have the rule over you, and submit yourselves: for they watch for your souls, as they that must give account, that they may do it with joy, and not with grief: for that is unprofitable for you. (Heb. 13:17)

> And we beseech you, brethren, to know them which labour among you, and are over you in the Lord, and admonish you; And to esteem them very highly in love

for their work's sake. And be at peace among yourselves. (vv. 12–13)

These exhortations require the leaders of the church to know the names of those they are responsible *for*, and it requires the members of the church to know the names of those they are responsible *to*. The requirements are gibberish otherwise.

Members have to remember their rulers. They have to remember their sermons. They must imitate their lives. They must render obedience, and they must be submissive. They must know those who labor in their midst. They must esteem them highly. And all of this means that they must know their names.

And what must elders do? They must rule, speak, and live lives worthy of imitation. They must joyfully watch over particular souls, as men who will give a reckoning. They must work and work hard, and they must admonish those who are erring. All of this requires them to know their parishioners' names. What would you think of your tax accountant if he said you owed a couple thousand dollars, and you said, "You sure?" and he said something like, "More or less." Accountants count. Shepherds *count*. Are they all here? Is everyone present? You always want the babysitters that you hire to have a firm grasp of how many children they start the evening with, and this should line up with how many they end the evening with.

These exhortations require discernment. You have to discern who is lazy and who is not. You have to discern who is unruly, and who is feeble. You have to discern the word of the Spirit, and you must have nothing to do with charlatans: "*God* told you, eh?" There is a true balance that has to be struck, which we can see in verse 21. Test everything, but do it with a certain spirit—a spirit that is eager to embrace whatever passes the test. In other words, you are to be a judge, but not a hanging judge. Be like the Ephesians in your hatred of the Nicolaitans, but do it without falling from your first love, the way the Ephesians did. Be like the Bereans, who searched the Scriptures diligently to see if these things were so, but who also received the word with great eagerness (Acts 17:11).

In the flesh, people who like to test things tend to be ornery; they like to see people crash and burn. In the flesh, people who are eager to hold fast to what is good tend to want everything to be good; everybody gets a participant ribbon. And these two errors feed off each other. The virtue we need to combat both of these opposing impulses is the grace of learning to lean on Scripture more than on our "own understanding." We want every personality to submit to all of Scripture, and not for every personality to use a set of verses to justify their own perspectives.

All of these traits are to be pursued and embraced in the light of the coming of Christ (vv. 23–24). And given how God has directed history, this means that you must pursue this lifestyle with your own death in view, or with the Final Coming of Christ in view. Going back to the previous point, those who love to hold people accountable must remember that the day is coming when *they* will be held accountable. And those who are allergic to every form of accountability must remember that the day is coming when they *will* be held accountable. "For we must all appear before the judgment seat of Christ; that every one may receive the things done in his body, according to that he hath done, whether it be good or bad" (2 Cor. 5:10).

2 THESSALONIANS

INTRODUCTION

The second epistle to the Thessalonians was likely written shortly after the first one, since it addresses many of the same sorts of issues. This beleaguered church was faced with hostility, was affected by an apocalyptic excitement, and also needed to deal with some of her members that were responding to this kind of thing poorly.

In the first chapter, Paul deals with the fierce opposition the Thessalonians had faced. In the second chapter, he discusses the "man of sin." And in the third, he provides his ethical application, which consists of a strong exhortation to *work*. In the face of hostility and persecution, and in the light of the apocalyptic era they were in, what should these Christians do? Well, obviously, they should keep hard at their work. They should not tolerate any slackers in their midst. They needed to stand fast. They needed to hold the traditions. They needed to receive the comfort of God, so that He would *establish* them in every good word and work.

God promises to deal with those who are harassing the church. He will settle the hash of the persecutors. He will take vengeance on those who do not know Him, and who do not obey the gospel (1:8). Notice that the gospel is a message to be obeyed. Notice also that Scripture does not teach that vengeance is wrong, but rather that vengeance is God's. Not only that, but the God who will judge all such things is the God who is in absolute control of everything. He is sovereign over their punishment, and He is sovereign over their sin as well. No matter how "out of control" everything might appear, remember that God is always in absolute control, and this includes the insanities of rebellious mankind.

One of the things we do at Christ Church is use suspension from the Lord's Table as a form of church discipline. This is not the same thing as excommunication, although a suspension could wind up with an excommunication. We have often been asked about this distinction between suspension and excommunication, and about our periodic use of "suspension" from the Lord's Supper. The biblical justification for that practice comes from this book.

In the Matthew 18 passage on church discipline, the process culminates with someone being turned out of the church, and treated as a heathen or a tax gatherer (Matt. 18:17). This is excommunication. But in this passage from Thessalonians, there are certain brothers who walk in a "disorderly" way. This disorderly walk consists of irresponsibility and laziness, but notice how Paul tells us to treat this category of sin. He says that we are to withdraw from such people (3:6), which would include eating with them. Like the virtuous woman in Proverbs, we are not to eat the bread of idleness (Prov. 31:27). We are therefore not to have table fellowship with such a person—but in the next breath he says that we must treat this person as a brother (3:15). This is something quite distinct from the Matthew 18 scenario. Suspension from the Lord's Supper opens up a way for a congregation to refrain from eating with a brother who is walking in a disorderly way, while at the same time still recognizing him *as* a brother.

Another theme of this letter is Paul's teaching about the "man of sin." Recall that the letters to the Thessalonians were written in the early fifties. Let me briefly tell you a story of what happened just over a decade earlier (AD 41), and ask yourself whether this was part of the backdrop in Paul's mind as he wrote the section on the man of sin.

Caligula was emperor, and he was out of his mind. He had become convinced of his own divinity, and ordered altars to be built and worship offered up to him. There was a city called Jamnia where some pagans did as they were instructed, but the city had a heavy Jewish population, and they demolished that altar. When Caligula heard of this, he was incensed and ordered an image of himself be placed in the Temple at *Jerusalem*. Petronius, the governor in Syria, was responsible for carrying this out, and he thought it was a crazy idea. Herod Agrippa (of all people) visited Rome, and was able to talk the emperor into what amounted to a revocation of the order. Then a letter arrived from Petronius, also asking the emperor to reconsider. This caused

Caligula to lose his temper again, and he revived the plan to set up the image in the Temple. He sent a letter to Petronius commanding him to commit suicide, but the letter did not reach the governor before news of the assassination of Caligula reached him. So *that* was a close call.

Now Paul says that the *parousia* of the Lord would not come unless some other things happened first. The man of sin, claiming to be divine, would declare himself to be God, and would do so in the Temple (2:3–4). The forces driving this folly were already at work (2:7). All of this would be destroyed by the Lord Jesus at His coming (*parousia*). So Paul's words here appear to reflect the events leading up to the judgments visited upon both Rome and Jerusalem in the years AD 68-70; but in chapter 2, we'll see how this fits with his description of the Final Coming.

Paul closes the letter by reminding the Thessalonians that, even in apocalyptic times, they should carry their own weight. How should you respond when unbelievers are attacking you? How should you deal with it when your theology tells you that you are living on the edge of a precipice? You should go out to the workshop. You should plant a tree. You should make dinner. "Now them that are such we command and exhort by our Lord Jesus Christ, that with quietness they work, and eat their own bread. But ye, brethren, be not weary in well doing" (3:12–13).

2 THESSALONIANS 1

EXTRAORDINARY GROWTH
One of the more difficult things for us to learn concerning our sanctification is the difference between repairs and growth. Both are involved in sanctification, but they are not at all the same thing. Imagine a potted flower that you have sitting on the window sill, flourishing there in the sunlight. Let us say that the cat knocks it over, shattering the clay pot. Now of course you repot it, and you hover over it carefully for a few days, and the plant seems to be doing okay. But then some weeks later, you are thrilled to see extra blossoms and more leaves, not to mention a couple of extra inches. This is all wonderful, but the thing to remember is that repotting the plant and nurturing the plant are two completely different activities. Unless you

had done the former, the latter would have been fruitless—but you need both.

> Paul, and Silvanus, and Timotheus, unto the church of the Thessalonians in God our Father and the Lord Jesus Christ: Grace unto you, and peace, from God our Father and the Lord Jesus Christ.
> We are bound to thank God always for you, brethren, as it is meet, because that your faith groweth exceedingly, and the charity of every one of you all toward each other aboundeth; So that we ourselves glory in you in the churches of God for your patience and faith in all your persecutions and tribulations that ye endure (2 Thess. 1:1–4)

This letter obviously has Paul as the main author, but like 1 Thessalonians, the salutation also includes Silvanus (Silas) and Timothy (v. 1). It is addressed to the church of the Thessalonians, a church which is in our Father God and in our Lord Jesus Christ (v. 1). The apostle extends a blessing to that church—grace and peace from the Father and Son (v. 2). Remember that all of Paul's epistles begin this way, with only two persons of the Trinity mentioned explicitly, and with grace and peace proceeding from them. My understanding is that this is because the "grace and peace" refers to the Spirit.

Paul then says that he is obligated (bound) to thank God for the Thessalonians, and to do so constantly (v. 3). This is fitting because their faith was growing "exceedingly," and their love for one another was "abounding." Their faith and their love were both overflowing the banks. Paul says that he glories in them "in the churches of God." What he means here is that he sets the Thessalonians in front of the other churches as a pattern or example for them to follow and imitate. They were setting this pattern in the midst of persecution and tribulations, doing so in "patience and faith" (v. 4).

Paul loves the use of superlatives. In the third verse, Paul says that their faith "groweth exceedingly" (v. 3). In the Greek, this is just one verb, not a verb and adverb, and to get the same effect in English, we would have to say that their faith was *hyper-growing*. He then goes on to say that their love for one another was abundant (v. 3). It was full, complete, increasing. Not only so, but they were doing this over a long haul—they were *enduring* their tribulations and persecutions (v. 4). It was an extended time, and it was full of trouble and affliction.

Put all this together, and what we see here is a genuinely antifragile congregation. They were able to thrive under adverse conditions. The more they went through, the more they flourished. Their faith was super-charged. Their love was running a ridiculous surplus. And they just kept on going. No wonder Paul would point to them as a remarkable congregation worthy of imitation. *We* should make a point of imitating them as well, even though it is over a great distance, both in centuries and miles.

Affliction, or tribulation, or trouble, or trial—whatever you want to call it—is not an *automatic* blessing. Remember what Jesus taught us about what can kill a plant dead: "And these are they likewise which are sown on stony ground;

who, when they have heard the word, immediately receive it with gladness; And have no root in themselves, and so endure but for a time: afterward, when affliction or persecution ariseth for the word's sake, immediately they are offended" (Mark 4:16–17).

This plant dies because of affliction and persecution, which is the same thing the Thessalonians were going through. But the Thessalonians were thriving, and these people were not. What is the difference? Jesus said that those who are offended and fall away are those who "have no root in themselves." The Thessalonians, on the other hand, were *in* the Father and the Son, and they have the Holy Spirit of God, grace and peace, *from* the Father and the Son. They were rooted well, and it showed.

For too many Christians, getting their Christian life squared away always seems to consist of replacing the broken pot. It is necessary to confess your sins, true. It is necessary to put things right with your brother, that is also true. It is necessary to do such things as a precondition of growth. But we must never forget that God calls us, not only to growth, but with the example of the Thessalonians before us, to *extraordinary* growth.

Your sanctification is not simply a matter of less malice, but of more love. Your growth is not simply a matter of less unbelief, but of more faith. Not less impatience, but more patience. Not less complaining merely, but more endurance. You don't want to be the gardener who gets so focused on pulling weeds that he forgets he is doing so in order to grow something else. It is supposed to be a flower garden, not a no-weeds dirt patch.

And there is only one place where it is possible for this to occur. We must be rooted in the Father and the Son, and we must be watered by the Spirit of grace and peace. When that happens, and when we as the people of God blossom, it fills the room with the aroma of Christ.

FLAMING JUDGMENT

The letter of 2 Thessalonians was written shortly after the first letter, probably just a few months later. This is based on the fact that both 1 and 2 Thessalonians are from Paul, Timothy, and Silas ("Silvanus" is another spelling of Silas). This creates a very narrow window for the letter to be written, sometime within the second missionary journey.

The purpose of 2 Thessalonians was to correct certain misunderstandings that the Thessalonians had about eschatology, and, some might argue, to create new misunderstandings for us. There *are* some challenges here.

> Which is a manifest token of the righteous judgment of God, that ye may be counted worthy of the kingdom of God, for which ye also suffer: Seeing it is a righteous thing with God to recompense tribulation to them that trouble you; And to you who are troubled rest with us, when the Lord Jesus shall be revealed from heaven with his mighty angels, In flaming fire taking vengeance on them that know not God, and that obey not the gospel of our Lord Jesus Christ: Who shall be punished with everlasting destruction from the presence of the Lord, and from the glory of his power; When he shall come to

be glorified in his saints, and to be admired in all them that believe (because our testimony among you was believed) in that day. Wherefore also we pray always for you, that our God would count you worthy of this calling, and fulfil all the good pleasure of his goodness, and the work of faith with power: That the name of our Lord Jesus Christ may be glorified in you, and ye in him, according to the grace of our God and the Lord Jesus Christ. (2 Thess. 1:5–12)

The steadfastness of the Thessalonians while facing persecution was evidence given by God that He was going to judge the wickedness of the persecutors (v. 5). Their courage was a manifest token that they were going to be counted worthy of the kingdom, on behalf of which they were suffering. It was obvious that it would be righteous for God to punish those who were troubling the saints, and to do it with real tribulation (v. 6). The saints will enter into rest, along with Paul and company, when the Lord Jesus is revealed from Heaven with His mighty angels (v. 7). That manifestation of Christ will bring the vengeance of flaming fire on those who do not know God, and who do not obey the gospel of Christ (v. 8). These people will be punished with everlasting destruction from the presence of the Lord, and from the glory of His power (v. 9)

When He comes, it will be so that He might be glorified in His saints (like the Thessalonians), and so that all who believed in response to Paul's message might be amazed at Him (v. 10). That was the reason why Paul continued to pray that God would count them worthy of their calling, and that they might fulfill all the good pleasure of His goodness, along with His work of faith with power (v. 11). The result will be a mutual glorification, Christ in them and they in Christ, all in accordance with grace (v. 12).

We must not forget that the man of lawlessness awaits us. In the next chapter of this book, we are going to be dealing with one of the most complicated eschatological passages in all of Scripture. There are probably twenty percent more interpretations than there are interpreters, and the whole thing is very sad. We have a few intimations of these difficulties in this chapter, and so some words about it now are in order.

As I understand it, our fixed anchor point is that all passages that address the general resurrection of the dead should be located at the end of history, when the Lord Jesus comes back to judge the living and the dead. That would include 1 Thessalonians 4:16–17, and it would also include 2 Thessalonians 1:7–10 and 2 Thessalonians 2:8. The challenge comes when we try to fit some of the surrounding statements on a timeline that appears to extend from the first century to the end of the world. Here are four basic positions outlined by Keith Mathison:

> The first option is to conclude that all the preliminary signs and the day of the Lord itself have already occurred. . . . A second option is to conclude that all of the preliminary signs have occurred, so there is now nothing preventing the coming of the day of the Lord, but the day of the Lord has not yet come. . . . A third option is to conclude that some of the preliminary signs

have either occurred or begun to occur, but since all of them have not yet occurred, the day of the Lord has not come yet.... A fourth option is to conclude that none of the preliminary signs have yet occurred, and therefore the day of the Lord has not yet come either.[3]

Like Mathison, my preference is for the third option. The day of the Lord has not yet come, and yet Paul appears to be making clear reference at places to the sorts of events that happened in the course of his lifetime. Remember that Caligula had attempted to have a statue of himself erected in the Temple at Jerusalem in AD 40, and only his murder prevented it. This attempt leads me to believe that he was a type of the man of sin . . . but not the man of sin himself. This is the *kind* of thing we are talking about.

But it would be a great mistake to miss the central point. We must not get caught up in the study of *when* the flaming judgment was going to come, and neglect the *fact* of a flaming judgment.

In this passage, we see who will be judged, and who will be vindicated. The Lord will appear in flaming fire, Paul says, and He will exact a strict vengeance. This vengeance will fall on those who do not know God, and it will fall on those who did not obey the gospel (v. 8). So what will be the nature of that damnation? The punishment is described here as an exclusion. They will be *shut out* from the presence of the Lord, and they will be *shut out* from the glory of His power (v. 9).

1. Keith A. Mathison, *From Age to Age: The Unfolding of Biblical Eschatology* (Phillipsburg, NJ: P&R Publishing, 2009), 532–533.

What is the gospel that commanded their obedience, obedience they refused to render? That gospel is the message that Christ died, was buried, rose again, and ascended into Heaven. From that place, He summons all men to believe in Him. The work we must do is the work of hearing and following Him on the basis of His death and resurrection.

When we contrast those who are shut out with those believers who admire Him (v. 10), we can see the very nature of damnation and salvation. In Heaven and Hell, we become what we have always been becoming. Men and women who love Christ will grow to love Him more and more, while men and women who hate Him will only sink deeper into that hatred.

2 THESSALONIANS 2

THE MAN OF SIN

And now we come to the challenging passage, the one I have been trying, in various ways, to warn you about. Who is the man of sin? What temple are we talking about? Who is the one impeding the man of sin for the time being? Good questions all.

> Now we beseech you, brethren, by the coming of our Lord Jesus Christ, and by our gathering together unto him, that ye be not soon shaken in mind, or be troubled, neither by spirit, nor by word, nor by letter as from us, as that the day of Christ is at hand. Let no man deceive you by any means: for that day shall not come, except there come a falling away first, and that man of sin

be revealed, the son of perdition; Who opposeth and exalteth himself above all that is called God, or that is worshipped; so that he as God sitteth in the temple of God, shewing himself that he is God. Remember ye not, that, when I was yet with you, I told you these things? And now ye know what withholdeth that he might be revealed in his time. For the mystery of iniquity doth already work: only he who now letteth will let, until he be taken out of the way. And then shall that Wicked be revealed, whom the Lord shall consume with the spirit of his mouth, and shall destroy with the brightness of his coming: Even him, whose coming is after the working of Satan with all power and signs and lying wonders, and with all deceivableness of unrighteousness in them that perish; because they received not the love of the truth, that they might be saved. And for this cause God shall send them strong delusion, that they should believe a lie: That they all might be damned who believed not the truth, but had pleasure in unrighteousness. (2 Thess. 2:1–12)

Paul pleads with the Thessalonians in the name of the Lord's coming (v. 1), that they not be unsettled through thinking that the final events were happening right then (v. 2). The day of Christ will not come unless the man of sin comes first (v. 3). This man of sin will set himself up in the Temple as God (v. 4). Paul had already explained all this to them on a previous occasion (v. 5). Some mysterious power is holding this lawless one back (vv. 6–7). Then the lawless one will be revealed in order to be destroyed by the

Final Coming of Christ (v. 8). He will be destroyed despite his ability to work miracles (v. 9). Those who love the truth will be saved in the truth, and those who love the lie will be damned in the lie (vv. 10–12).

What are the challenges here? The description appears to refer to the Final Coming of Christ, which is still in our future. The coming of the Lord (*parousia*) could be His coming in judgment on Jerusalem, except that the phrase "our gathering to him" is used. And the man of sin who exalts himself as God will be consumed by the Spirit of the Lord's mouth and destroyed by the brightness of the Lord's coming. All this certainly sounds like the final eschaton.

But then what is meant by "the temple of God" here? The Jewish Temple was destroyed in AD 70. So if the man of sin set himself up there, then these events would be in the distant past and not a description of the Final Coming. This is one of the reasons why dispensationalists argue that the Temple has to be rebuilt. Another argument is that the Temple is the Christian church, and that this false teacher who claims to be God is something like a wicked pope.

Realize that Paul is telling the Thessalonians *not* to think that these events are right on top of them (v. 2). Don't be unsettled, he says. A number of other things need to happen first. There needs to be an apostasy, a falling away (v. 3). There needs to be a miracle-working false teacher (v. 9), one who claims to be God and enthrones himself in the Temple (v. 4).

At the same time, Paul does argue that the spirit of all such things is already manifesting itself in his day (v. 7). He says that there is an unnamed external power that is restraining the outbreak of this lawless one (vv. 6–7). He says that the mystery of iniquity is already at work (v. 7), and is pushing back against that which restrains it.

So here is my understanding of all this (Mathison's third option in the previous chapter). The event that happened just a decade or so before this, when Caligula attempted to set up a statue of himself in the Temple, was the *kind* of thing Paul was talking about, but was not the event itself. It was the spirit that was already active, but was not the final convulsion of mankind's sin. That is yet in our future, and Paul teaches us that it will run along the same lines. The advance of the kingdom of God is all part of *the same long war*. It is a protracted conflict, and it is all the same conflict. We are two thousand years after this prediction from Paul, but when Jesus preached to the spirits who were rebellious at the time of Noah (1 Pet. 3:19–20), He was 2,400 years after the Flood. And it was all still relevant. History is a river, not a string of ponds.

The issues are therefore perennial, and they come down to every man and every woman, every boy and every girl. Those who have their pleasure in unrighteousness, and who reject the truth because they do not love it, are going to be sent something that lines up with what they love and hate. This passage says that God will send them a strong delusion so that they should believe a lie. And why is this? It is because they loved the lie. It is because they did not love the truth.

Salvation is a function of loving the truth. Damnation is a function of loving a lie, preeminently the lies you tell yourself. Self-deception is the prince of all deceptions. The wrath of God is seen in this, when God gives people over to what they have loved all along.

The one who causes these delusions to evaporate is a preached Christ. And He is a preached Christ only because He is a crucified Christ, and a buried Christ, and a risen Christ. He is the truth, and He is preached. Do you love Him? If not, then the strong delusion is already resting upon you. If so, then you are loving the truth, by which you are saved.

EVERLASTING CONSOLATION

This is a passage in which we can clearly see the basic Pauline cast of mind. How does the apostle Paul think about the relationship of gospel truth and gospel living? How do the two fit together?

> But we are bound to give thanks alway to God for you, brethren beloved of the Lord, because God hath from the beginning chosen you to salvation through sanctification of the Spirit and belief of the truth: Whereunto he called you by our gospel, to the obtaining of the glory of our Lord Jesus Christ. Therefore, brethren, stand fast, and hold the traditions which ye have been taught, whether by word, or our epistle. Now our Lord Jesus Christ himself, and God, even our Father, which hath loved us, and hath given us everlasting consolation and good hope through grace, comfort your hearts, and stablish you in every good word and work. (2 Thess. 2:13–17)

Paul acknowledges that he has an obligation to be grateful for the Thessalonians (v. 13). They were brothers beloved of the Lord, and his gratitude includes the fact that God had chosen them for salvation, using the sanctification by the Spirit and their belief in the truth (v. 13). God called them to that salvation by means of the gospel (v. 14), so that they might come to obtain the glory of the Lord Jesus Christ (v. 14). We enter into that glory through the cross—if we die with Him, we will also live with Him. That being the case, they were instructed to stand fast (v. 15). Hold on to the traditions you have received, the apostle says, whether you received them verbally or through an epistle (v. 15). He then wraps up this exhortation with a benediction. May the Lord Jesus and God the Father—who has loved us, and given us everlasting consolation and good hope through grace (v. 16)—comfort your hearts and establish you in every good word and work (v. 17).

So what are we to make of apostolic tradition? This section of Thessalonians is one of two places in the Bible where tradition is mentioned positively (see also 1 Cor. 11:2). Everywhere else it is negative. Jesus rebukes the Pharisees for setting aside the commands of God for the sake of human traditions (Mark 7:8–9, 13). Paul warns the Colossians to beware of philosophy, vain deceit, traditions of men, and the rudiments of the world (Col. 2:8). Paul states that in the time of his unbelief, he had been "exceedingly zealous" for the traditions of his fathers (Gal. 1:14), which was not a good thing. The apostle Peter reminds his readers that they had been rescued from their vain way of life received by tradition from their fathers (1 Pet. 1:18). Protestant Christians are therefore justified in giving a wary stink eye to any exorbitant claim made on behalf of tradition.

But here, tradition is lauded. Fortunately, we are given two important clues about the content of this apostolic tradition. First, in our text, Paul says that "the traditions" were what they had been taught, whether by spoken or by written word. In other words, we should expect the oral traditions, which we do not have, to be very much like the written traditions, which we *do* have.

And second, in the next chapter, Paul gives us a sample of what he means by *tradition*:

> Now we command you, brethren, in the name of our Lord Jesus Christ, that ye withdraw yourselves from every brother that walketh disorderly, and *not after the tradition which he received of us*. For yourselves know how ye ought to follow us: for we behaved not ourselves disorderly among you; Neither did we eat any man's bread for nought; but wrought with labour and travail night and day, that we might not be chargeable to any of you. (2 Thess. 3:6-8)

So what is the apostolic tradition? Work hard. Show up on time. Don't call in sick when you aren't. Don't be a malingerer. In short, the apostolic tradition is *not esoteric at all*. Change your oil every three thousand miles. Rotate your tires.

Earlier I mentioned the Pauline cast of mind. And here it is.

When Christians live as Christians should, this is an occasion for gratitude to be rendered to God. When *we* live right, we should thank *Him*. The initiative in salvation lies with God. God is the one who chose us for salvation. And why? Because *He* wanted to. He chose the slaves to sin that He was going to liberate, and His method of liberation was to give the holiness of the Spirit and the faith that enabled us to believe the truth. When we abandon all attempts to hang onto our own glory, surrendering all of it in a God-glorifying gospel, what is the result? He calls us by that gospel, and He calls us up into the obtaining of the glory of the Lord Jesus. *When we surrender the glory of man, He invites us up into the glory of God.*

These things being the case, we should contemplate them, and respond in an appropriate way. What is that? Stand fast in the truth. Hold to the apostolic tradition, which means that you should get a job. When you stand up straight in the gospel, the Father and the Son, who called you to that gospel in the first place, will preserve you there. God will do this because He loves you. He has given you an everlasting consolation. He has given you good hope through grace. He will comfort your hearts. And then what will He do regarding the rest of your life? He will *establish* you in every good word and work.

God tells human masters not to govern through threatening. This is what *He* is like. In the gospel, God's Spirit governs us without threatening, without condemnation.

There is consolation here indeed. Consider what this established work actually is. There is hope and there is comfort. The grace of God is abundantly present. But we must take care not to import our own "traditions" into this picture. God's comfort is not a Big-Rock-Candy-Mountain kind of comfort. Notice that God does not promise to float you like a feather on a zephyr up to Heaven. It is not *that* kind of a good time.

He establishes us in every good word and work, and work is what? It is *work*. The promised glory of a golden harvest does not erase the fact that there are months of work out in another kind of golden reality, the heat of the summer sun.

This is the way of Christ. It is the apostolic tradition. Salvation is all of grace, which is why we all work so hard. Salvation is all of Christ, for all of life, which is why it sanctifies all of our work.

2 THESSALONIANS 3

PATIENCE IN WORK THAT WAITS
Although the church at Thessalonica was a remarkably healthy church, it could not be said that there were *no* disorders there. At the conclusion of this second letter, Paul turns to some practical matters concerning their lives together. Right at the center of those matters is the question of work, along with what to do with people who aren't working.

> Finally, brethren, pray for us, that the word of the Lord may have free course, and be glorified, even as it is with you: And that we may be delivered from unreasonable and wicked men: for all men have not faith. But the Lord is faithful, who shall stablish you, and keep you from evil. And we have confidence in the

Lord touching you, that ye both do and will do the things which we command you. And the Lord direct your hearts into the love of God, and into the patient waiting for Christ.

Now we command you, brethren, in the name of our Lord Jesus Christ, that ye withdraw yourselves from every brother that walketh disorderly, and not after the tradition which he received of us. For yourselves know how ye ought to follow us: for we behaved not ourselves disorderly among you; Neither did we eat any man's bread for nought; but wrought with labour and travail night and day, that we might not be chargeable to any of you: Not because we have not power, but to make ourselves an ensample unto you to follow us. For even when we were with you, this we commanded you, that if any would not work, neither should he eat. For we hear that there are some which walk among you disorderly, working not at all, but are busybodies. Now them that are such we command and exhort by our Lord Jesus Christ, that with quietness they work, and eat their own bread.

But ye, brethren, be not weary in well doing. And if any man obey not our word by this epistle, note that man, and have no company with him, that he may be ashamed. Yet count him not as an enemy, but admonish him as a brother.

Now the Lord of peace himself give you peace always by all means. The Lord be with you all.

The salutation of Paul with mine own hand, which is the token in every epistle: so I write.

The grace of our Lord Jesus Christ be with you all.
Amen. (2 Thess. 3:1–18)

Paul concludes this letter to the Thessalonians by requesting prayer, as he often does. He prays that the word of the Lord might run freely, and be glorified, as was already happening in Thessalonica. And in order for this to occur, he requests that prayers be offered up for *him* (v. 1). When the gospel runs freely, it does so through human agency. Paul requests prayer for their deliverance from unreasonable and wicked men, the kind who do not have faith (v. 2). God is faithful, and will protect the Thessalonians (v. 3). Paul has confidence in the Thessalonians, that they will follow his instructions (v. 4). He asks God to direct them into the love of God and into a patient waiting for Christ (v. 5). So what does that look like?

The Thessalonians were to withdraw from any disorderly brothers (v. 6). Paul's entourage had set the example in this for them (v. 7). Paul paid for his own food (v. 8). He could have required support, but preferred to provide an example (v. 9). He had set the standard for them while he was there—non-workers should be non-eaters (v. 10). A report had come to Paul that the Thessalonian church had some busybodies, who lived in a disorderly way (v. 11). He commands those people to get a job (v. 12). He then exhorts them all not to get tired of doing the right thing (v. 13). If any are uncooperative, then mark and shun them (v. 14), doing it in a brotherly way (v. 15). Then comes the benediction: may the God of peace grant you His peace (v. 16). Paul signs off with his own hand, as was his custom (v. 17). May the grace of God bless all of you (v. 18), and *amen*.

What does patient waiting look like? This chapter begins on a strong gospel note, and then takes a surprising turn. May the word of the Lord run free. Pray for gospel proclamation. Pray we be guarded against those who would persecute us for our preaching. May God guide you into a greater love for God and into a patient waiting for Christ to come.

Patient waiting for the Final Coming does not look like a complicated system of charts and graphs calculating when the end will come. Still less does it look like some poor sap sitting on his roof because he thinks those charts and graphs are his ultimate truth. No. What does patient waiting look like? *It looks like working hard at your job, and being dedicated to your vocation.*

Everything Paul teaches here is aimed at this sort of Christian industry. Waiting for Christ looks like withdrawing from the disorderly (v. 6a). Working hard is an apostolic tradition (v. 6b). Paul set an example of hard work (vv. 7–8), an example he intended for them to follow (v. 9). Waiting for Christ follows the command not to feed certain people (v. 10). Waiting for Christ means that you learn to distinguish productive work from busy work (v. 11). The disorderly are often busybodies, meaning that lazy people *can* scurry around with all the latest news. The Greek word for *that* indicates a man bustling around the edges of all the hard work, carrying a shovel, and wearing an official reflector vest.

We wait for Christ by working without a lot of fanfare or noise (v. 12). We wait for Christ by sustaining that work over time (v. 13), and not getting tired of it. And last, we wait for Christ by being willing to give brotherly admonitions to others about the quality of their work (vv. 14–15).

It is necessary for us to learn how to admonish a brother who is not walking in an orderly way. A church that does not practice church discipline is a church with an immune system collapse. Not disciplining against heresy means there is no protection for the body from error, and not disciplining against moral failure means there is no protection for the body from immorality. The two things that mark a true church garden are Word and sacrament, and without the fence of church discipline, such a garden will not last for long.

There are gradations of this discipline. Sometimes the discipline is conducted by means of warnings from the pulpit. Sometimes it is conducted by a personal admonition. Other times, when a person's life is disorderly and not disciplined rightly, it is conducted by avoiding that person. That is what we see here. And then in severe cases, we follow the process laid out in Matthew 18:15–20.

But notice that the end result of the Matthew 18 process is that the person is treated as a heathen or tax collector. In other words, this person is ejected from the church, excommunicated. There are other people, as here, who are avoided, but are nevertheless admonished *as brothers* (v. 15). As mentioned before, this is why our church polity has the category of *suspension*, a point well shy of excommunication.

In the gospel, God gives *Himself*. Here at the end of the letter, Paul prays that the God of peace will give the

Thessalonians peace. Reasoning by analogy, may the God of grace give us grace, may the God of love give us love, may the God of joy give us joy. In short, may the God of our salvation grant us salvation, which He does by *giving us Himself*.

God so loved the world that He gave . . . what? John 3:16 tells us that He gave us His Son. And what did His Son give us after He returned to Heaven? He gave us His Spirit. What does God do for His people? He always gives us Himself.